Musical Families

Opening Night

with the Woodwind Family!

by Trisha Speed Shaskan   illustrated by Robert Meganck

PICTURE WINDOW BOOKS
a capstone imprint

Special thanks to our advisers for their expertise:

Rick Orpen, PhD, Professor of Music, Gustavus Adolphus College
Terry Flaherty, PhD, Professor of English, Minnesota State University, Mankato

Picture Window Books
151 Good Counsel Drive
P.O. Box 669
Mankato, MN 56002-0669
877-845-8392
www.capstonepub.com

Editor: Jill Kalz
Designer: Lori Bye
Art Director: Nathan Gassman
Production Specialist: Jane Klenk
The illustrations in this book were
created digitally.

Printed in the United States of America in North Mankato, Minnesota
032010
005740CGF10

All books published by Picture Window Books
are manufactured with paper containing at least
10 percent post-consumer waste.

Library of Congress Cataloging-in-Publication Data
Shaskan, Trisha Speed, 1973–
Opening night with the woodwind family! / by Trisha Speed Shaskan ;
illustrated by Robert Meganck.
p. cm. — (Musical families)
Includes index.
ISBN 978-1-4048-6042-1 (library binding)
1. Woodwind instruments—Juvenile literature. I. Meganck, Robert. II.
Title.
ML931.S52 2011
788.2'19—dc22
2010001075

We're called woodwinds because we need air, or "wind," to make music. Woodwind musicians usually blow across a reed attached to a mouthpiece. Clarinets, oboes, bassoons, and saxophones have reeds. Flutes don't. When air moves through woodwinds, we sing!

reed

mouthpiece

4

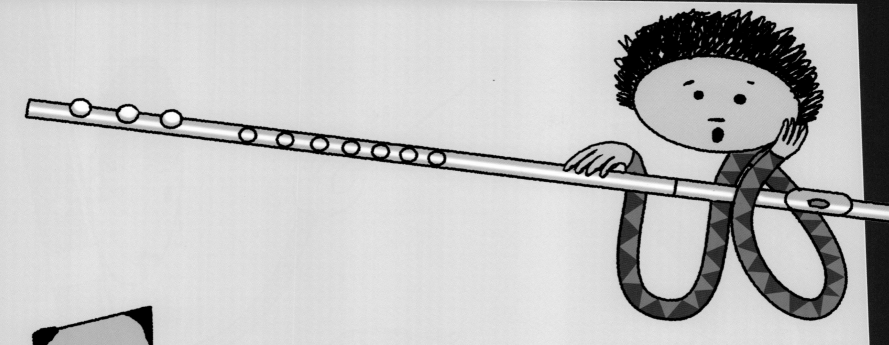

Our family name is a bit confusing. We're called woodwinds, but not all of us are made of wood. Flutes are made of metal. So are saxophones.

My family is getting ready for a big concert tonight at Orchestra Hall. We've been practicing all summer. Mom says I can be a tricky instrument to play. But she loves how I sound sweet and sad all at once.

To play an oboe, a musician blows air across a double reed. The ends of the reed vibrate against each other between her lips. To make different sounds, the musician presses down on keys. The keys cover holes in the oboe's body.

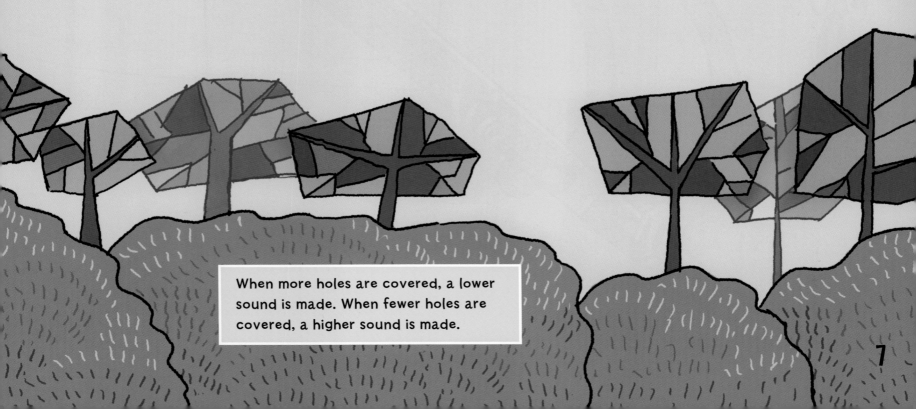

When more holes are covered, a lower sound is made. When fewer holes are covered, a higher sound is made.

My mom has a double reed too. She can be just as tricky to play as I am. She's the lowest sounding instrument in our family. I think she's also the most talented.

Bassoons are heavy. To help hold the instrument, a musician sits on a strap connected to the bassoon's base.

She can sound HAPPY, then SAD.

She plays HIGH, nasally notes

and LOW, buzzing notes.

My dad is one cool saxophone. He used to have his own jazz band. Like Mom, Dad can play high, happy notes, and low, mysterious or sad notes.

He can whisper.

He can SHOUT.

He can laugh, cry, and surprise.

Jazz is a style of music that began in the southern United States. African-Americans were the first to play jazz.

10

To play a saxophone, a musician often sits in a chair, with the instrument at his right side.

My sister, Clara, and I kind of look alike. But clarinets have their own sound. Clara is a great storyteller. She doesn't hit the highest notes or the lowest notes, but she does hit all the notes in between. And there are a lot of them!

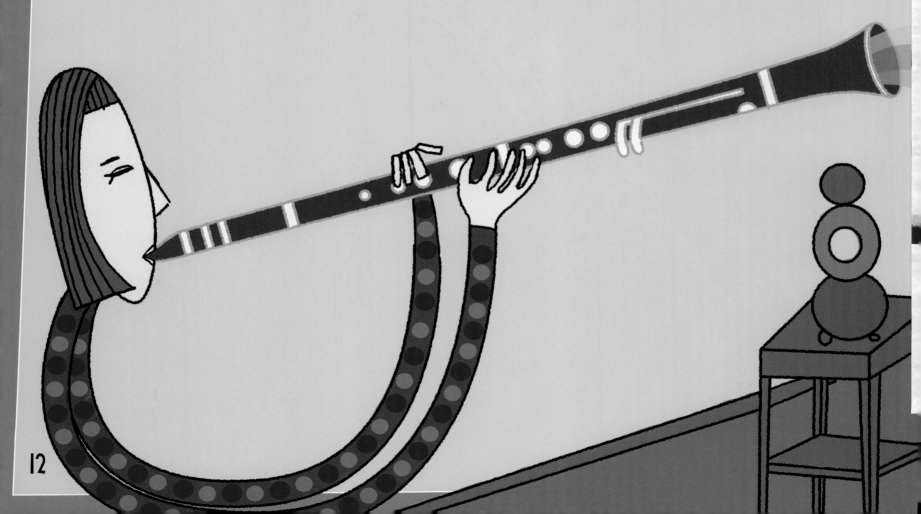

Clarinets, like saxophones, have only one reed. When a musician blows into a clarinet, the reed vibrates against the mouthpiece and makes sound.

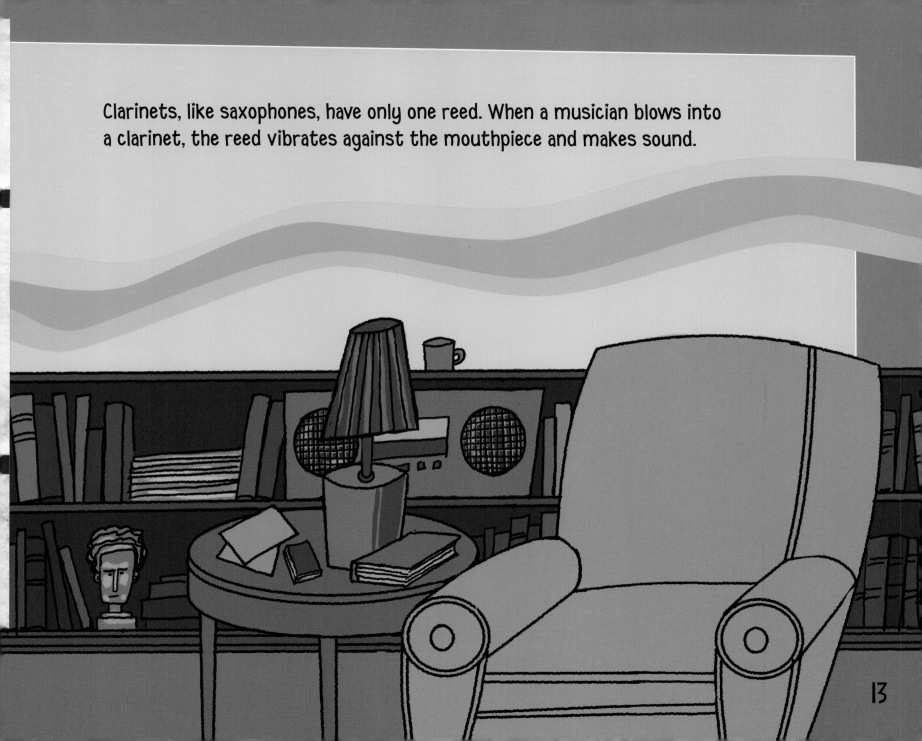

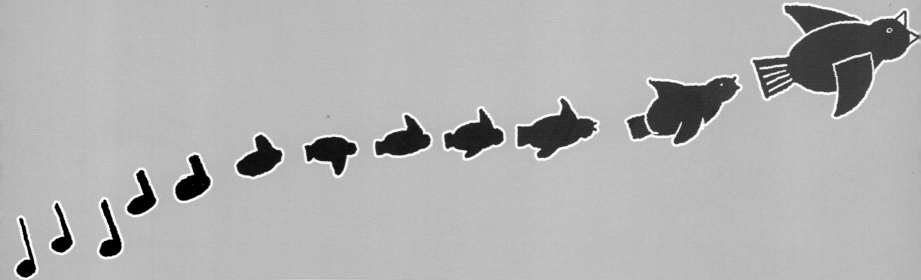

Flint has the highest voice in our family. When he practices, it's magical. His notes lift and dance into the air like birds.

To play a flute, a musician holds the instrument out to the side. Then he blows across an oval-shaped hole. It's like blowing into a bottle.

Later in the afternoon, my family meets in the living room. I'm not the biggest or flashiest instrument, but I'm pretty important. I start by holding one special note.

The oboe is the one instrument to which all the other instruments in an orchestra are tuned.

Once everyone is tuned, we practice together for the last time. Then we get out our cleaning and repair kits. We have to be in tip-top shape for tonight's concert.

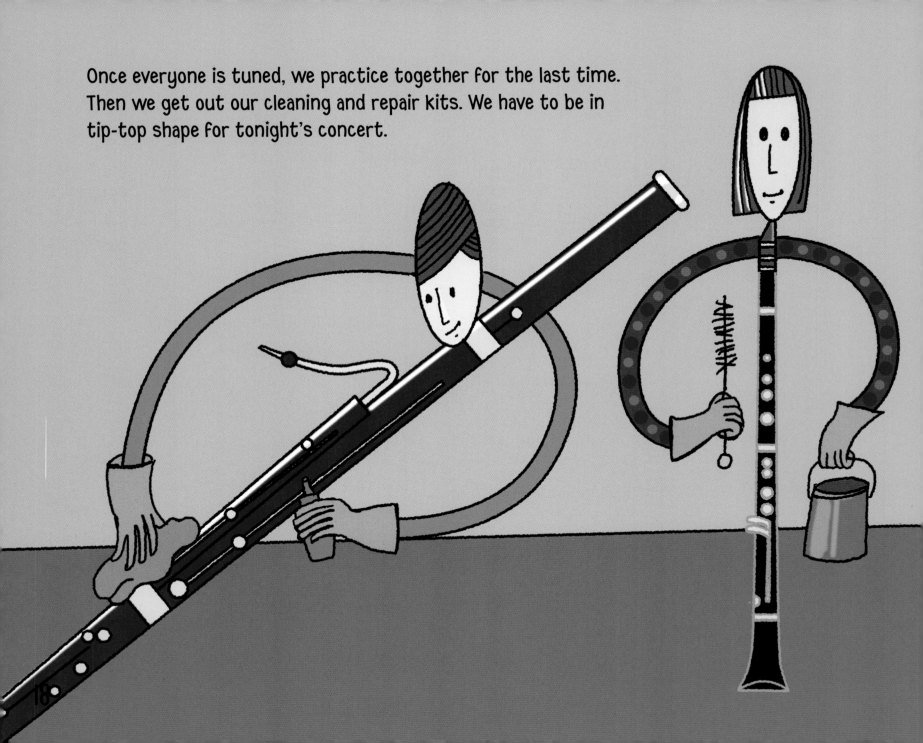

A musician's breath makes a woodwind instrument wet inside. Musicians must dry their instruments before putting them away, or mold could grow.

We're finally here!

Orchestra Hall!

I play my one special note, and all the other instruments tune themselves to me.

Saxophones play an important part in concert bands, marching bands, and jazz bands. But they aren't part of a standard orchestra.

The lights dim. The hall quiets. The conductor lifts her arms, and we play.

The crowd goes wild!

They love us. We'll be back for another show soon.

Glossary

conductor—the person who leads an orchestra

mouthpiece—the part of a wind instrument into which a musician blows

musician—a person who plays music

orchestra—a group of musicians who play together on various instruments, especially violins and other string instruments

pitch—how high or low a sound is

reed—a small piece of cane (a hollow, woody plant stem) attached to the mouthpiece of some instruments to help them make sound

rhythm—a pattern of beats

tune—to change to the right pitch

vibrate—to move back and forth very quickly

Fun Facts

A musician who plays a woodwind instrument may be called a bassoonist, a clarinetist, a flutist, an oboist, or a saxophonist.

The flute is one of the oldest instruments in the world. In Ancient Egypt, flutes were made of cane (a hollow, woody plant stem) or metal.

One of the most famous jazz saxophonists of the 1940s was Charlie "Yardbird" Parker. He was known for his amazing solos (music played by just one instrument).

To Learn More

More Books to Read

Helsby, Genevieve, with Marin Alsop. *Those Amazing Musical Instruments.* Naperville, Ill.: Sourcebooks, 2007.

Knight, M.J. *Brass and Woodwinds.* Musical Instruments of the World. North Mankato, Minn.: Smart Apple Media, 2006.

Koscielniak, Bruce. *The Story of the Incredible Orchestra.* Boston: Houghton Mifflin Co., 2000.

Internet Sites

FactHound offers a safe, fun way to find Internet sites related to this book.
All of the sites on FactHound have been researched by our staff.
Here's all you do:
Visit *www.facthound.com*
FactHound will fetch the best sites for you!

Index

Look for all the books in the Musical Families series:

Around the World with the Percussion Family!
The Brass Family on Parade!
The Keyboard Family Takes Center Stage!
Opening Night with the Woodwind Family!
The String Family in Harmony!